Yellow Umbrella Books are published by Capstone Press
151 Good Counsel Drive, P.O. Box 669, Mankato, Minnesota 56002
www.capstonepress.com

*Library of Congress Cataloging-in-Publication Data*
VanVoorst, Jennifer, 1972–
    Make it move! / by Jennifer VanVoorst.
    p. cm.
    Summary: Simple text and photographs introduce simple machines and give
examples of their everyday use.
    ISBN 0-7368-2939-3 (hardcover)—ISBN 0-7368-2898-2 (softcover)
    1. Simple machines—Juvenile literature. [1. Simple machines.] I. Title.
TJ147.V28 2004
621.8—dc21                                                    2003007741

**Editorial Credits**
Editorial Director: Mary Lindeen
Editor: Jennifer VanVoorst
Photo Researcher: Scott Thoms
Developer: Raindrop Publishing

**Photo Credits**
Cover: Ariel Skelley/Corbis; Title Page: Image Source/elektraVision; Page 2: EyeWire;
Page 3: Rim Light/PhotoLink/PhotoDisc; Page 4: John Foxx; Page 5: Joseph Sohm/
ChromoSohm Inc./Corbis; Page 6: Randy Miller/Corbis; Page 7: Getty Images/Taxi;
Page 8: Daemmrich Bob/Corbis Sygma; Page 9: DigitalVision; Page 10: Corbis; Page 11:
Image Source/elektraVision; Page 12: Brian A. Vikander/Corbis; Page 13: EyeWire;
Page 14: Image Source/elektraVision; Page 15: Corbis; Page 16: Keith Brofsky/Brand X
Pictures

1  2  3  4  5  6  09  08  07  06  05  04

# Make It Move!

by Jennifer VanVoorst

Consultant: Paul Ohmann, PhD, Assistant Professor,
Department of Physics, University of St. Thomas

Yellow Umbrella Books

an imprint of Capstone Press
Mankato, Minnesota

# Simple Machines

How can you make things move?
Use a machine! Some machines
have many parts.

Other machines are called simple machines. Simple machines are all around you.

# Pulleys

A pulley is a simple machine. It makes lifting heavy things easier.

Cranes use pulleys to lift heavy objects. You can use a pulley to raise a flag.

# Levers

Levers are simple machines, too.
Levers help move heavy loads.
A wheelbarrow is a lever.

A bottle opener is a lever.
A seesaw is a lever, too!

# Inclined Planes

An inclined plane is a simple machine. An inclined plane is a slant. A ramp is an inclined plane.

Stairs are an inclined plane.
A slide is an inclined plane, too.

# Wedges

A wedge is a simple machine.
Wedges can cut objects.

An axe is a wedge.
A knife is a wedge.
Teeth are wedges, too!

# Wheels and Axles

Wheels and axles are simple machines. An axle is a rod attached to a wheel. This wagon has four wheels and two axles.

A windmill has a wheel and axle. A wheelchair has wheels and axles, too!

# Screws

A screw is a simple machine. Spirals on the screw help it move into an object.

A bolt is a screw.
A lid is a screw.
A lightbulb is a screw, too!

# Make It Move!

Simple machines are everywhere!
What can they help you move?

# Words to Know/Index

**axle**—a rod in the center of a wheel; the wheel turns around the axle; pages 12, 13

**inclined plane**—a slanted surface; an inclined plane makes it easier to raise and lower heavy loads; pages 8, 9

**lever**—a bar used to lift or move objects; pages 6, 7

**machine**—a tool that makes it easier to move things; pages 2, 3

**pulley**—a rope around a wheel with a grooved rim; a pulley makes it easier to lift or move objects; pages 4, 5

**screw**—a rod with a thread around it; a screw is a simple machine that is used to hold objects together; pages 14, 15

**wedge**—a wood, metal, or plastic object that is thin at one end and thick at the other; wedges are used to cut things; pages 10, 11

Word Count: 215
Early-Intervention Level: 15